The Story of Chocolate

Katie Daynes

Illustrated by
Adam Larkum

Reading consultant: Alison Kelly
University of Surrey Roehampton

Contents

Chapter 1

Chocolate drinkers

A thousand years ago,
chocolate was a big secret.
Only a few people drank
it and nobody ate it.

The first chocolate drinkers were farmers who lived by the rainforest in central America.

The rainforest was a jungle full of tropical plants, wild animals and creepy crawlies. It was also home to the small cocoa tree that grew strange, bright pods.

4

Monkeys knew all about
the pods. They liked to
break them open and suck
out the sweet, white pulp.
Then they spat out the
bitter beans that were
in the middle.

If a bean landed on an
earthy patch of forest floor, it
grew into another cocoa tree.

5

One day, a farmer copied
the monkeys and tasted a pod.
"Yum!" he cried, sucking
the pulp. "Yuck!" he added,
spitting out a bean. Soon
everyone was sucking
pulp and spitting beans.

But then, some villagers
noticed a delicious smell,
drifting up from a pile of
rotting beans.

Over the next few months, the farmers discovered a way to capture this smell by turning the beans into a drink.

They let the beans rot for a few days under banana leaves...

then put them out to dry in the hot sun.

Next, they roasted the beans over a fire...

ground them into a paste...

and stirred in water and spices. They called their new drink *chocol haa*. It tasted very bitter, but they liked it.

8

To avoid hiking into the jungle for pods, the farmers planted cocoa trees in their own fields.

The farmers were members of a huge group of people called Mayans. Before long, *chocol haa* – or chocolate – was an important part of Mayan life.

Mayan kings and priests began to drink it every day. They liked the froth best.

At Mayan weddings, the bride and groom showed their love for each other by exchanging five cocoa beans.

In fact, people were so enchanted by the cocoa tree, they painted it on everything – their pots, their mugs and even their walls.

But preparing cocoa beans was hard work and took weeks. Most people were only allowed to drink chocolate as a special treat.

Cocoa beans became so valuable they were used as money. You could buy a rabbit for ten beans and a slave for one hundred.

Chapter 2

Learning the secret

Hundreds of years later, a group of merchants arrived in a Mayan village. They had journeyed for days to find exotic goods for their emperor.

13

The merchants belonged to a fierce group of people called Aztecs. To avoid trouble, the Mayans offered them some of their precious beans.

When the Aztecs had learned the chocolate secret, they served a cupful to their emperor. He was delighted.

"Perfect!" he cried. "A cool, refreshing drink that doesn't make you drunk." And he ordered all his warriors to drink chocolate before they went into battle.

Where the Aztecs lived it was too cold to grow cocoa. So, they had to buy their beans from the Mayans and carry them all the way home.

The Aztec emperor, Montezuma, was crazy about chocolate. He kept the royal warehouses piled high with cocoa beans. Sometimes he ordered 50 cups of chocolate a day, thinking they would make him richer and wiser.

Oh, go on then, just one more.

But poorer people could only dream about chocolate.

16

Over time, a legend grew up about where chocolate first came from.

"Once upon a time, the world had no chocolate," said the storytellers. "Then Quetzalcoatl, the god of farming, appeared from paradise with a cocoa tree."

Quetzalcoatl was the Aztecs' hero. They built him grand temples and left him chocolate drinks as gifts.

But other countries had their eyes on the Aztecs' riches. Chocolate wouldn't stay a central American secret for long...

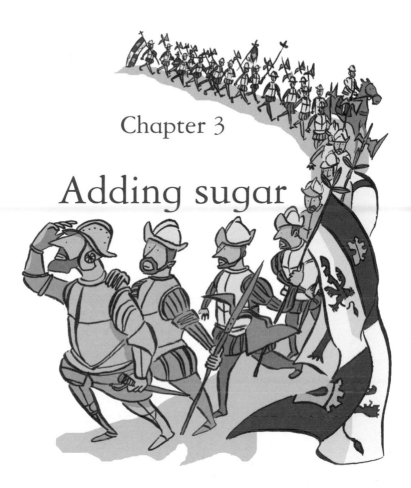

Chapter 3

Adding sugar

In 1519, a Spanish explorer named Hernán Cortés set out with an army to fight the Aztecs.

After many battles, Emperor Montezuma wanted to make peace and he invited Cortés to court. He gave Cortés his first taste of chocolate.

Cortés liked the chocolate but he still conquered the Aztecs. In 1528, when Cortés sailed home, his sacks were bursting with Aztec treasure... including cocoa beans.

Back in Spain, Cortés served the chocolate drink to his friends. They decided it tasted better hot and with lots of sugar. It was so good, they kept it to themselves.

But the Spanish prince, Philip, soon heard about the drink. A group of monks took some visitors from central America to meet him... and they brought a tub of chocolate paste as a gift.

Prince Philip was hooked. He made sweet, hot chocolate the drink of the Spanish court.

Chocolate gossip spread fast. People in Europe were talking about it long before they had even seen a potato.

But turning cocoa beans into chocolate paste took a long time and it was very expensive.

Only rich Europeans had enough money to buy the drink. They would sit around in cafés, sipping hot chocolate and talking about the weather.

Chapter 4

Chocolate machines

It wasn't until inventors came up with the steam engine that things changed. Suddenly, lots of goods could be made more easily – including chocolate.

Factories were set up all over Europe and turning cocoa beans into chocolate drinks became big business.

Before long, the drink had stopped being just a handmade treat for the rich.

In 1847, an English chocolate maker, Francis Fry, decided there could only be one thing better than drinking chocolate...

and that was eating it. His problem was how to turn chocolate paste into solid bars.

In Holland, Coenraad Van Houten provided half the answer. He invented a press that separated chocolate paste into brown cocoa powder and yellow cocoa butter.

Fry noticed that cocoa butter hardened as it cooled. "Maybe I can use that to make solid chocolate," he thought.

He stirred warm cocoa butter into his chocolate paste...

added three scoops of sugar...

poured the mixture into square tubs...

and waited. Slowly, it went hard. Fry had invented the world's first chocolate bar!

In no time, factories were making bars of rich, dark chocolate. They called it *delicious chocolate to eat.*

Meanwhile, in Switzerland, there lived a candlemaker named Daniel Peter. But candles were going out of fashion and he was losing money.

When he fell in love with a chocolate maker's daughter, he had a brilliant idea.

"I'll make chocolate instead!"

By now, there was lots of competition in the chocolate business. Peter needed to make his bar special.

He tried adding milk, but that made the chocolate too runny. Peter was stuck. Luckily, Henri Nestlé lived next door and he knew a lot about food.

Are you sure about this?

Nestlé earned his living making baby food. He soon found a way to thicken Peter's chocolate mix.

In 1883, Peter won a gold medal for his new, creamy chocolate recipe. Milk chocolate was a hit.

Chapter 5

Tasty inventions

By the 20th century, people had learned how to make milk chocolate smoother, creamier and even more tasty. We still use the same methods today.

First, the chocolate mixture is put through heavy rollers, to squeeze out every lump.

Then an enormous vat, invented by Rodolphe Lindt, is used to blend the mixture into a smooth, velvety paste.

The chocolate is cooled and warmed and cooled and warmed until it has a glossy shine. Finally, it is poured into trays to set.

For years, eating-chocolate was only made in solid bars. But Milton Hershey, an American chocolate maker, thought bars were boring.

36

In 1907, he tried squirting glossy chocolate into little peaks. When the peaks hardened, he wrapped each one in foil to make them look more exciting.

It wasn't long before factories were making chocolates in all shapes and sizes.

The next challenge was to mix chocolate with other scrumptious ingredients.

In 1912, an American candy maker called Howell Campbell was feeling adventurous. He stirred peanuts, caramel and marshmallows into glossy, melted chocolate.

Then, he spooned gooey blobs of the mixture onto a tray. As the chocolate set, the blobs hardened and Campbell took his first bite.

It's deliciously gooey!

He called his invention the Goo Goo Cluster. It was one of the first mixed chocolate snacks, and an instant success.

That same year, a Belgian chocolate maker, Jean Neuhaus, made another leap in chocolate history. He invented hard chocolate shells that could hold soft fillings.

After stuffing them with a creamy, nutty mix, he sealed them up with more chocolate.

From then on, there was no stopping the chocolate makers. Silky caramel, chewy toffee, nutty almonds, creamy vanilla – you name it, they added it.

Factories churned out hundreds of different chocolate snacks, while smaller companies made amazing chocolates by hand.

Chapter 6

Chocolate families

Some of today's chocolate companies are gigantic. But most of them began as small family businesses.

In 1824, John Cadbury opened a shop in England. Along with tea and coffee, he sold his own drinking chocolate.

It was so popular, Cadbury set up a cocoa and chocolate factory. Now Cadbury's drinks and chocolate bars are sold across the globe.

In 1911, Frank and Ethel Mars set up a business in America, selling homemade butter-cream candies. Their big break came in 1923 when Frank invented a malted milk chocolate bar.

He made a fluffy, malty nougat...

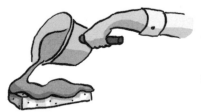

topped it with caramel...

and coated it in milk chocolate.

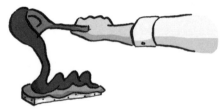

Then, in 1941, their son Forrest developed another sweet idea: sugar-coated chocolate drops that wouldn't melt in your hand.

An American, named Bruce Murrie, gave Mars some money for the project. So they called their new chocolates M&M's.

Here's to Mars and Murrie!

Today, you can buy the Mars family's chocolates almost anywhere in the world and they're nothing like the Mayans' bitter drink.

When the Mayans first caught a whiff of rotting cocoa beans, they knew they had found something exciting. But they had no idea how popular chocolate would become.

A chocolate recipe

Glossy chocolate sauce

Ingredients:
100g (½ cup) dark (semi-sweet) chocolate chips
2 tablespoons golden syrup (corn syrup)
15g (1 tablespoon) butter
2 tablespoons water

What to do:
Put all the ingredients
in a small saucepan and
heat them gently. Keep
stirring until they mix into
a smooth, glossy sauce.

Be careful!
The saucepan
and sauce will
be hot.

Eat the sauce poured over slices
of banana or scoops of ice
cream. You could sprinkle
it with marshmallows or
nuts if you like.

47

With thanks to Catherine Atkinson for the recipe
and John Davidson-Kelly for helpful advice

Series editor: Lesley Sims
Designed by Russell Punter
and Katarina Dragoslavic

First published in 2004 by Usborne Publishing Ltd., Usborne House,
83-85 Saffron Hill, London EC1N 8RT, England. www.usborne.com
Copyright © 2004 Usborne Publishing Ltd.